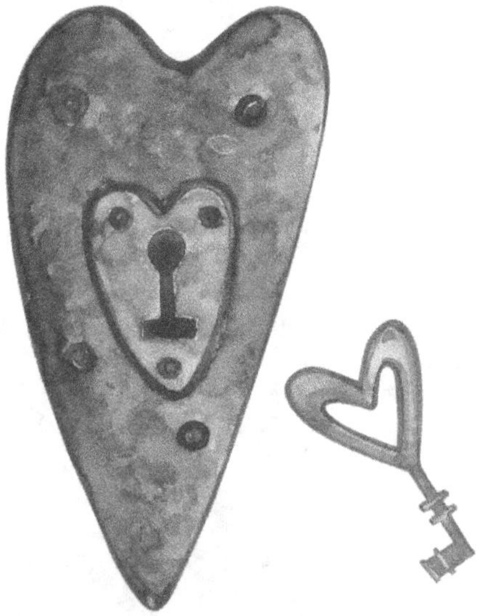

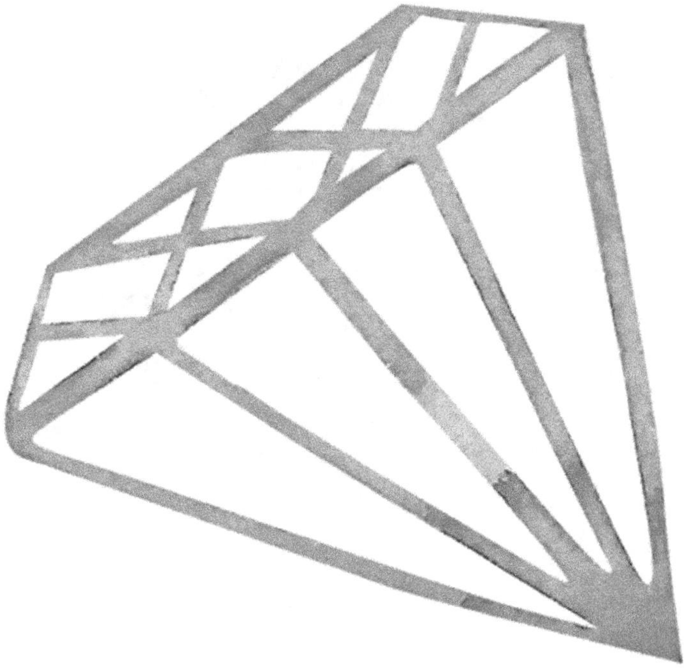

you
+
me
=
love

i love you

love you

LOVE

you are loved

love is all you need

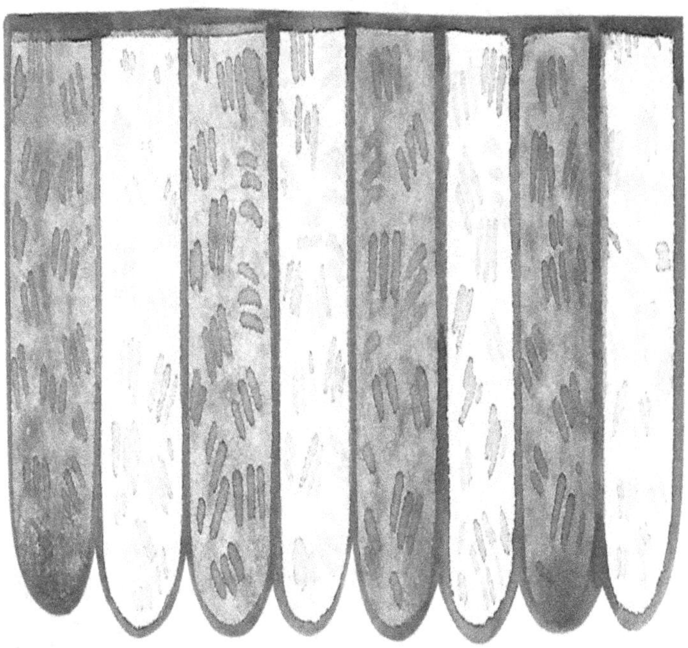

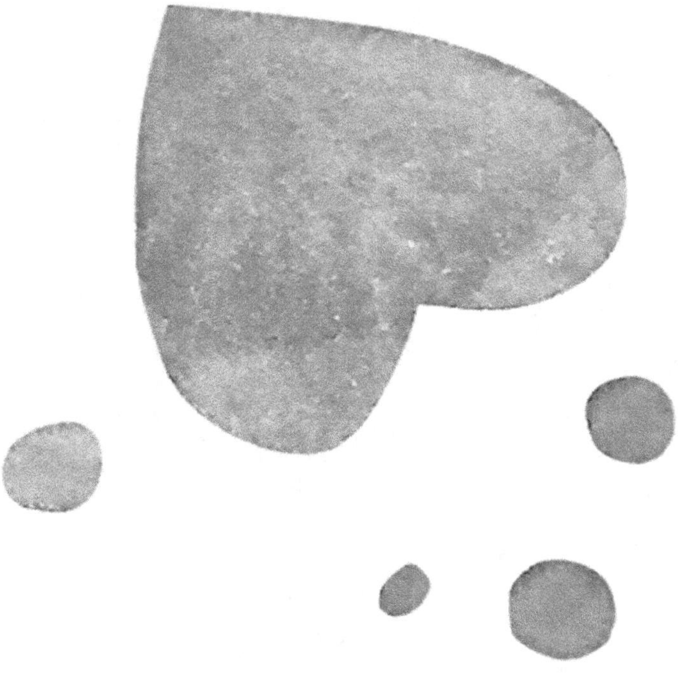

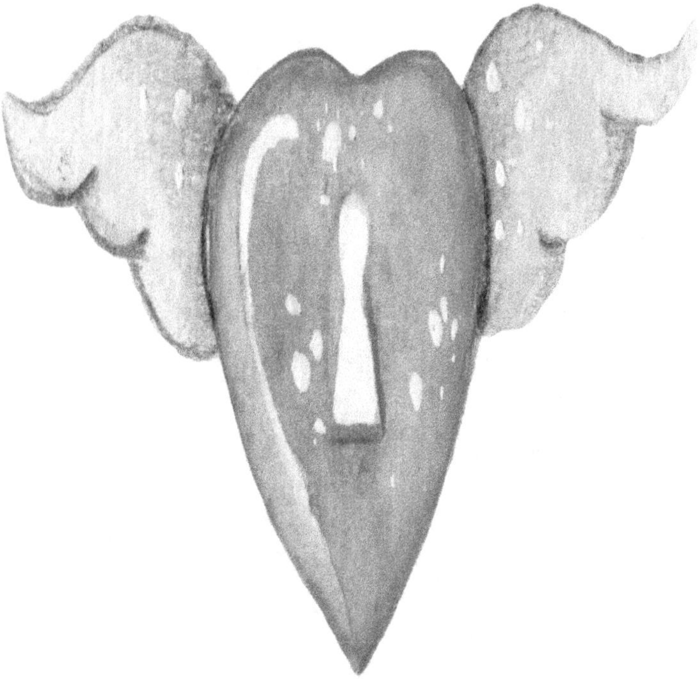

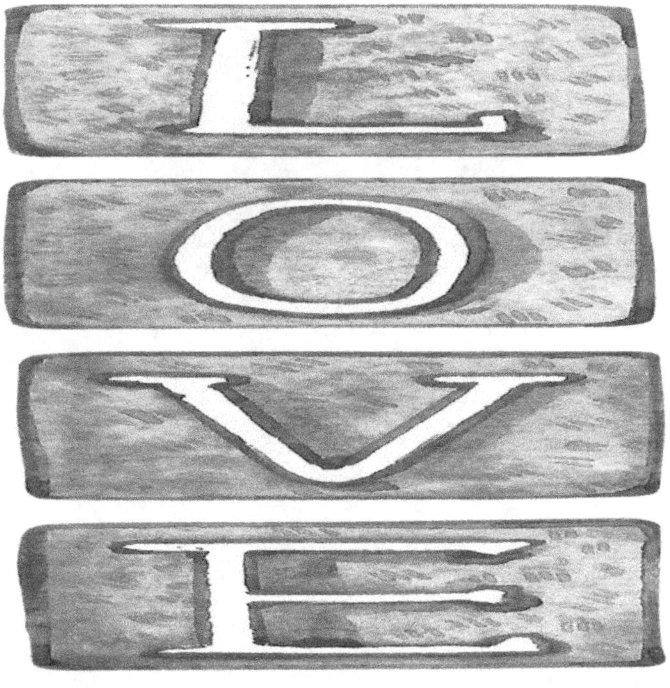
L
O
V
E

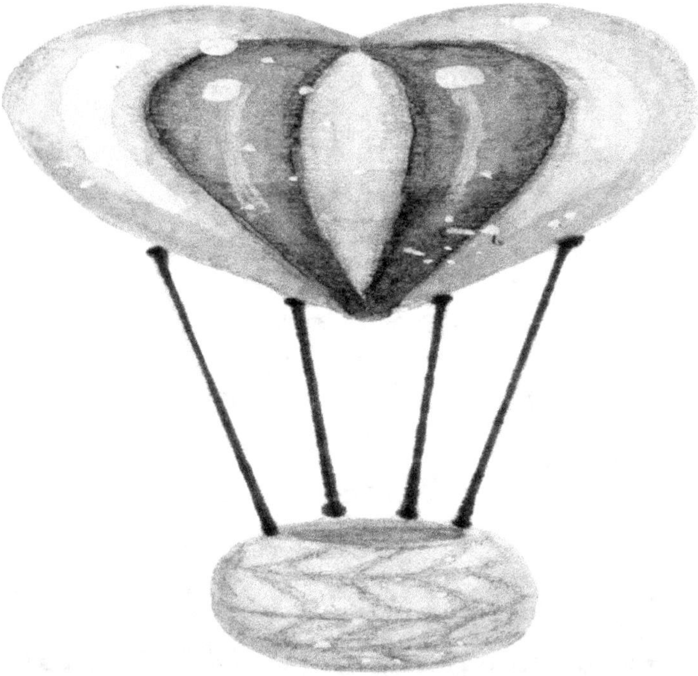

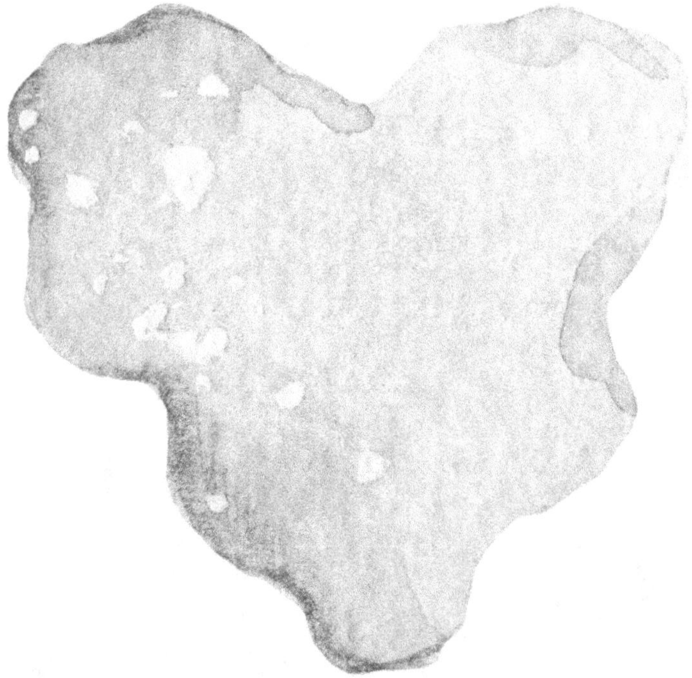

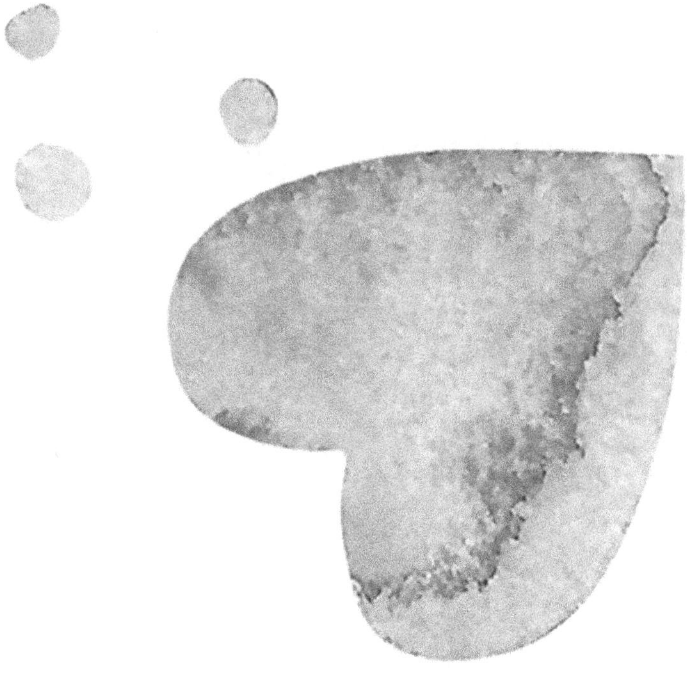

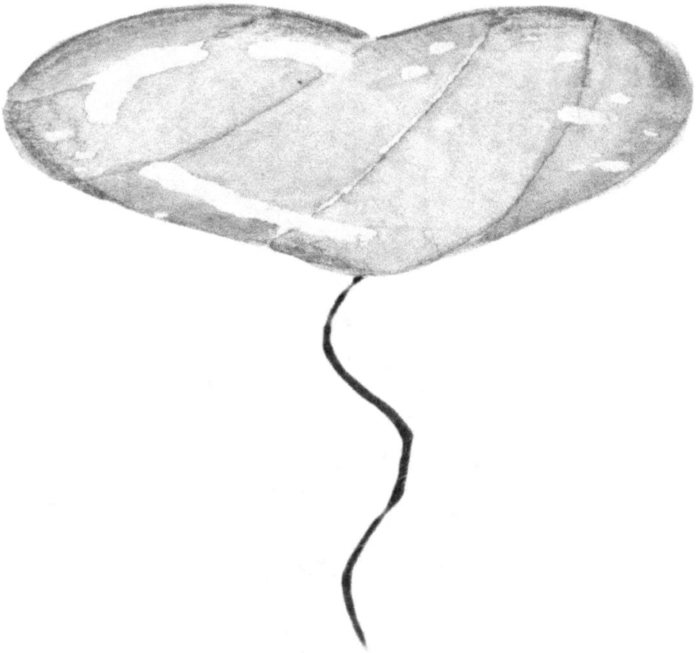

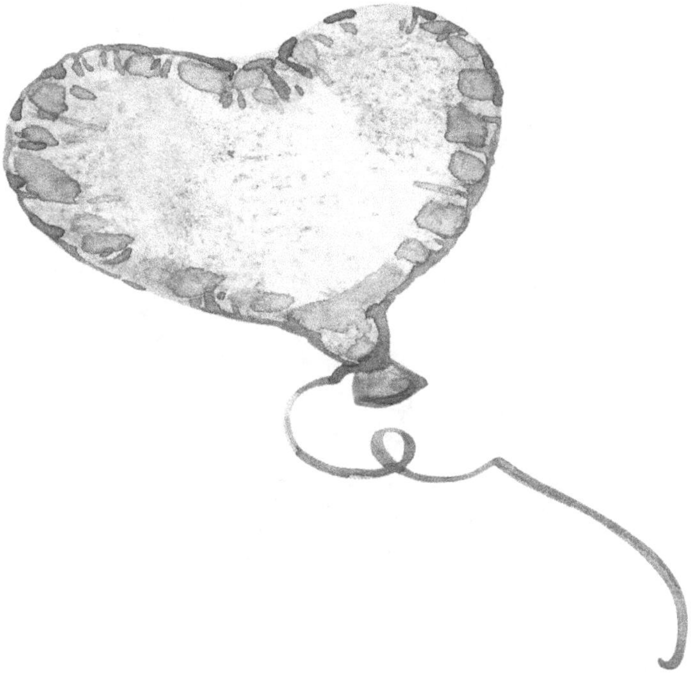

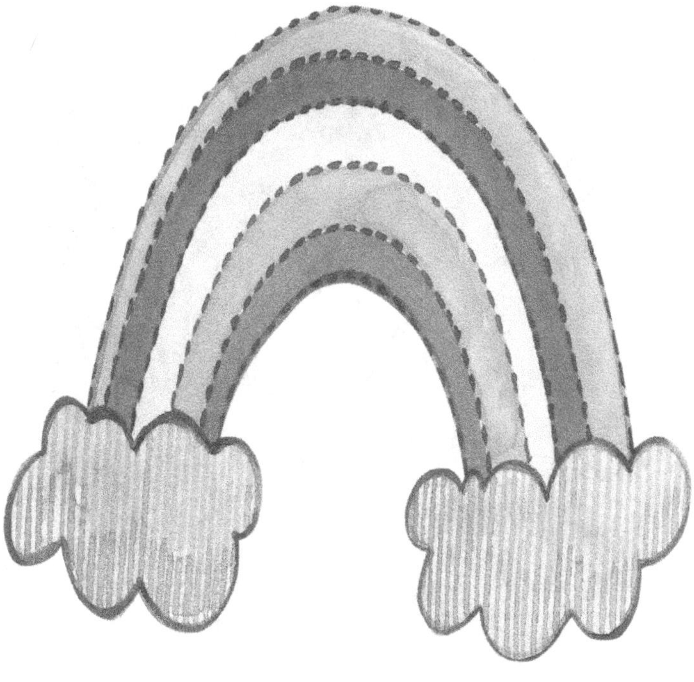

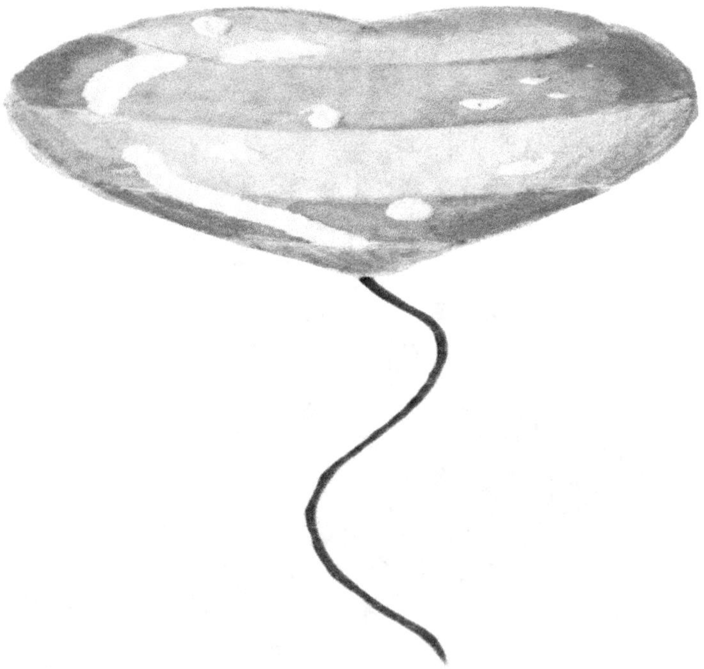

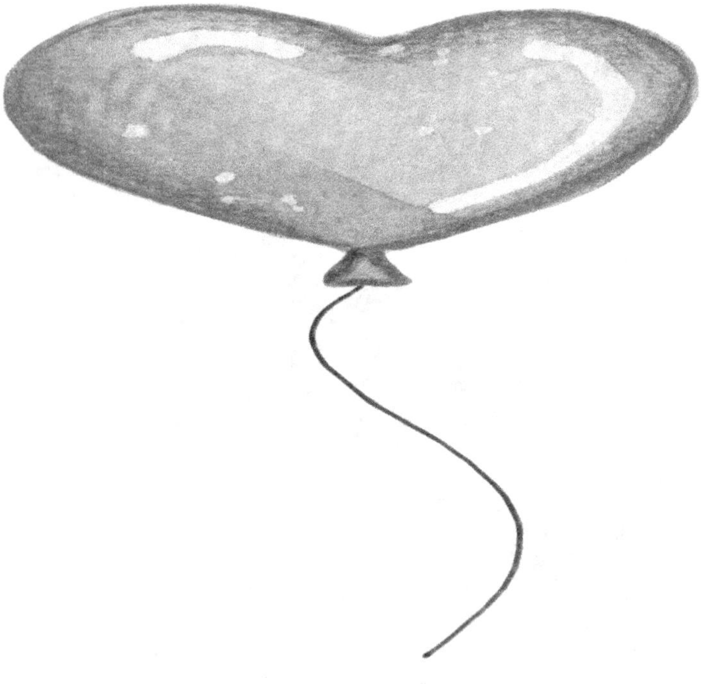

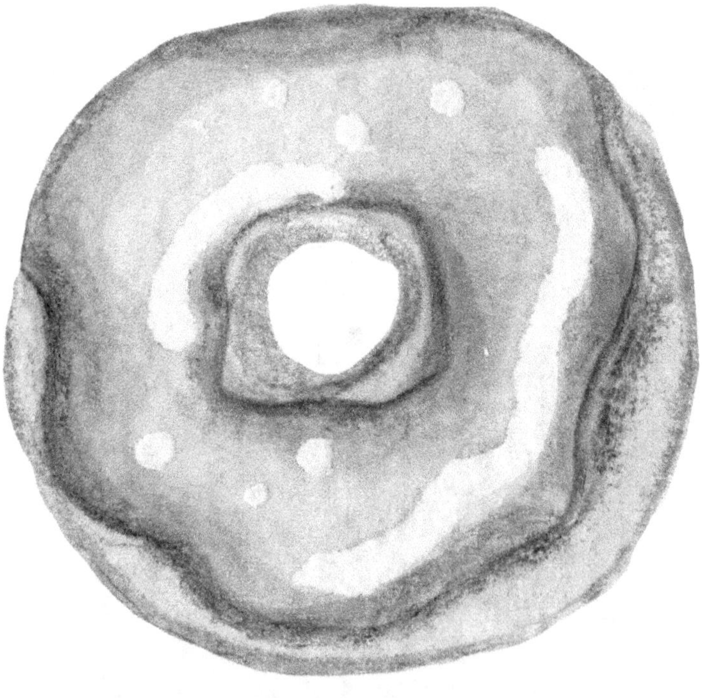

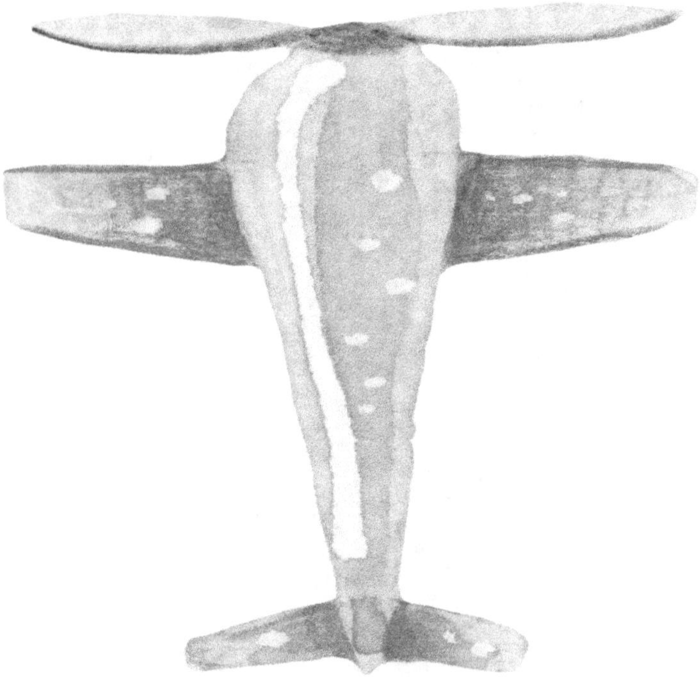

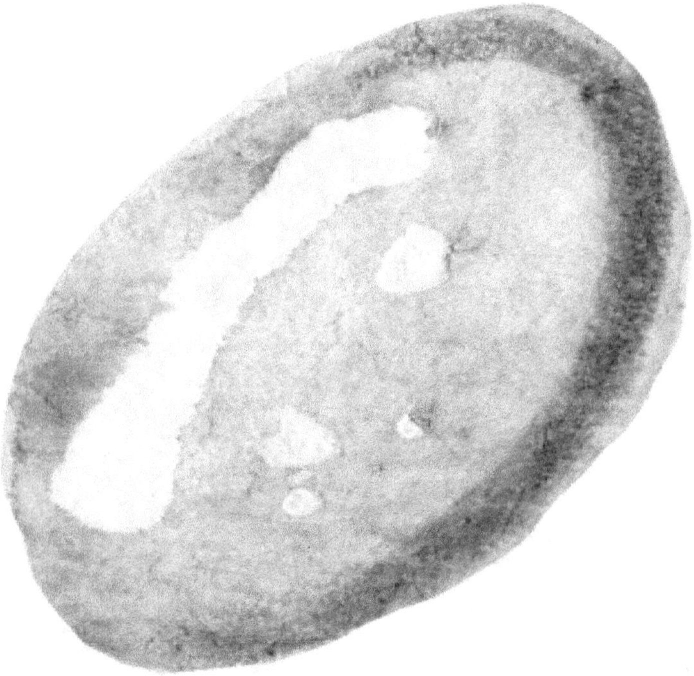

love

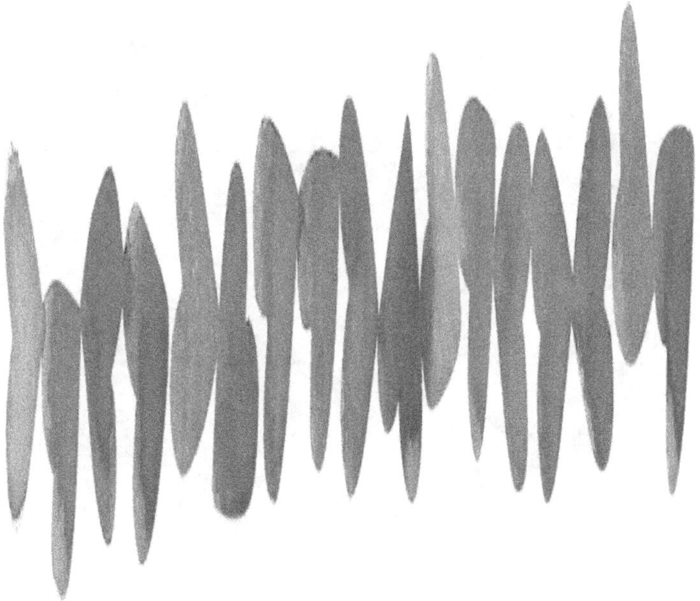

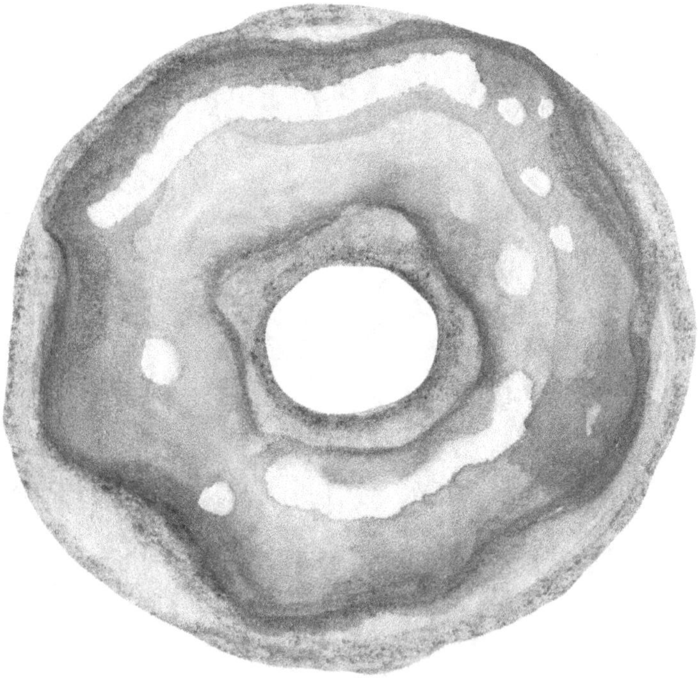

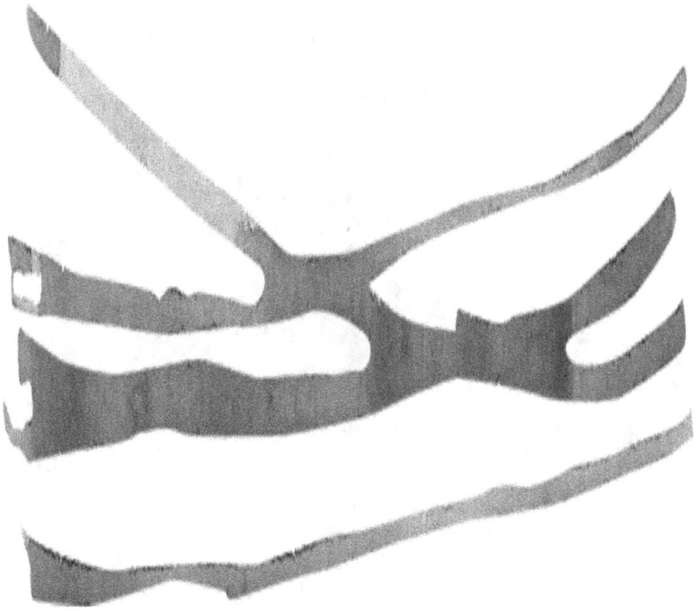

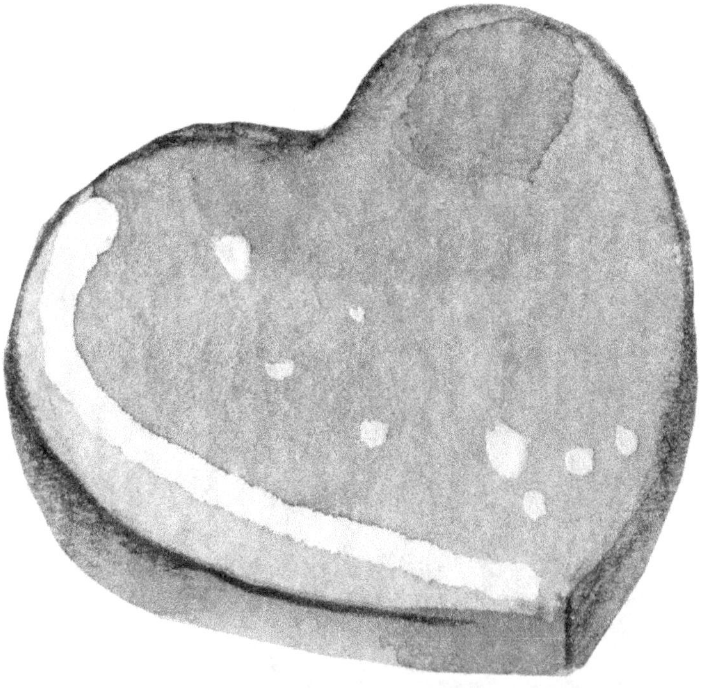

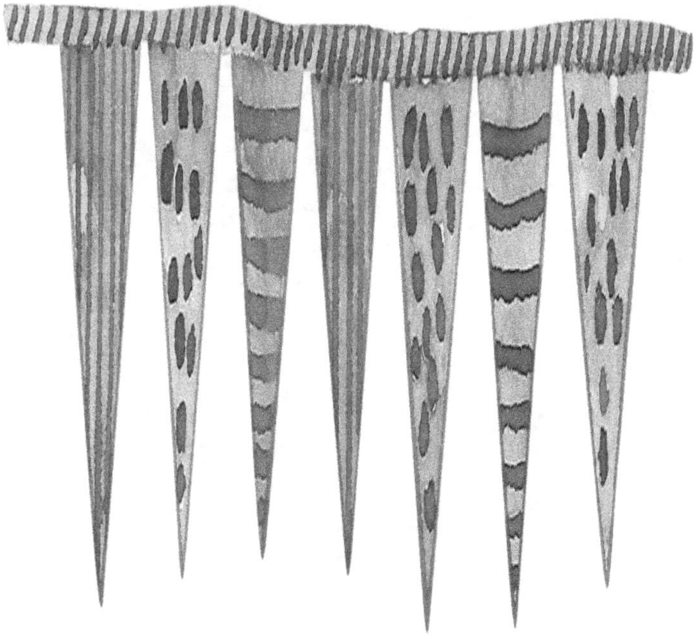

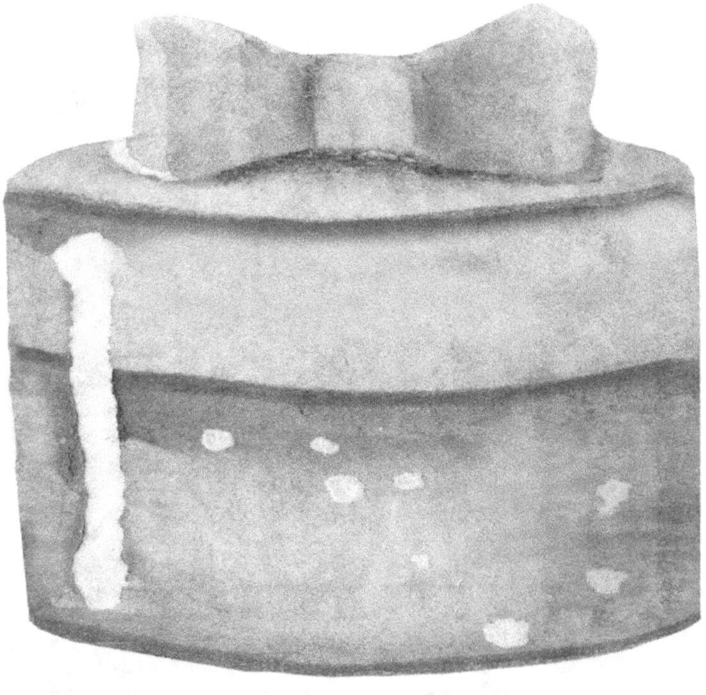

YAY

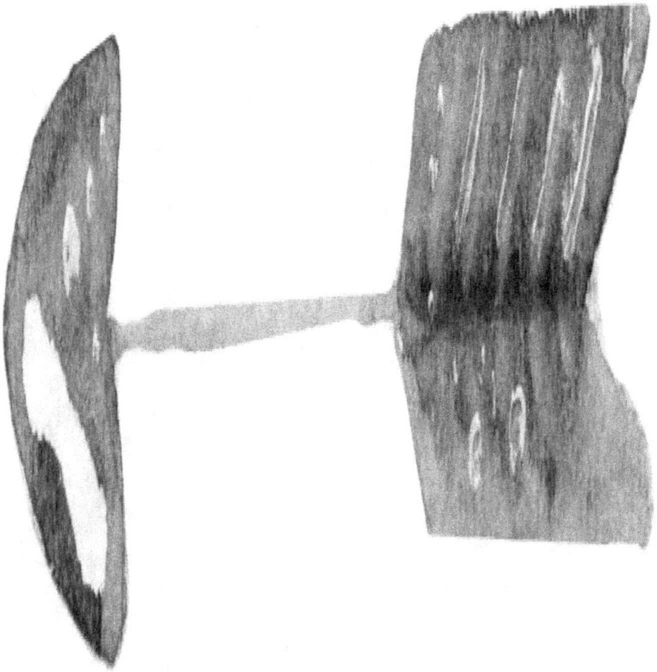

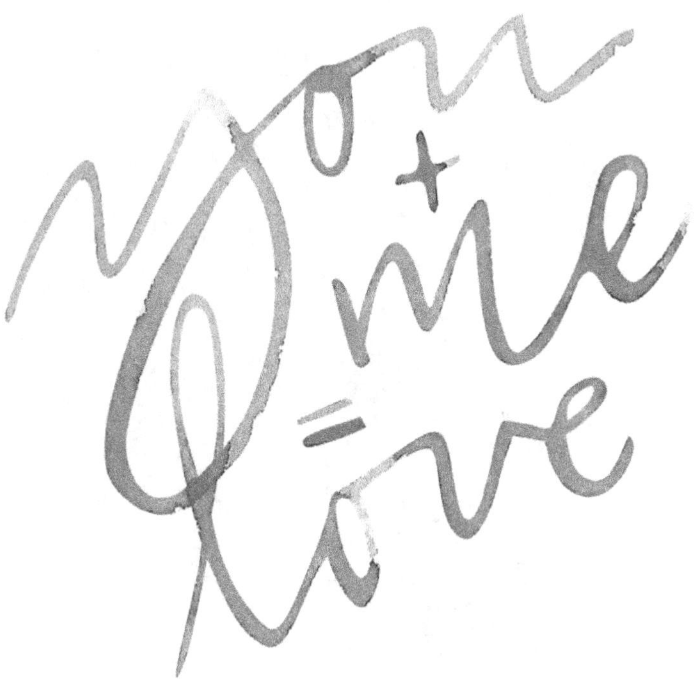
you
+
me
=
love

believe
IN
Love

love

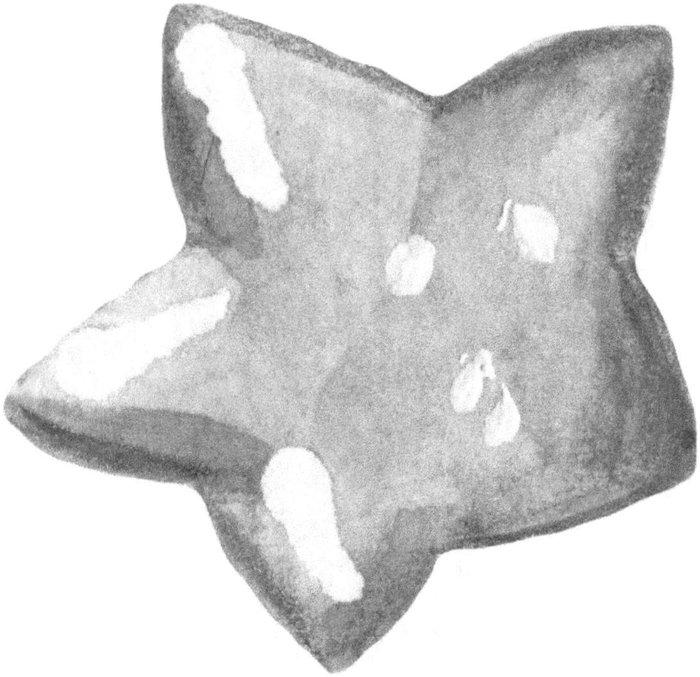

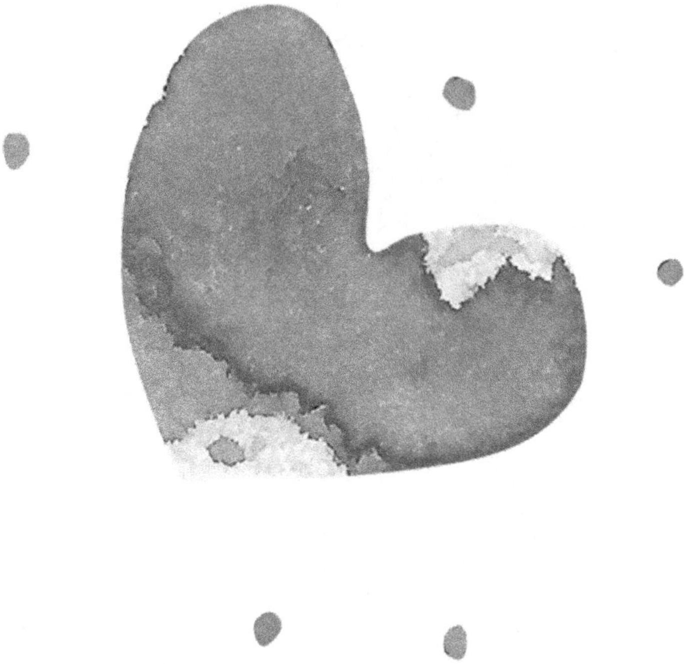

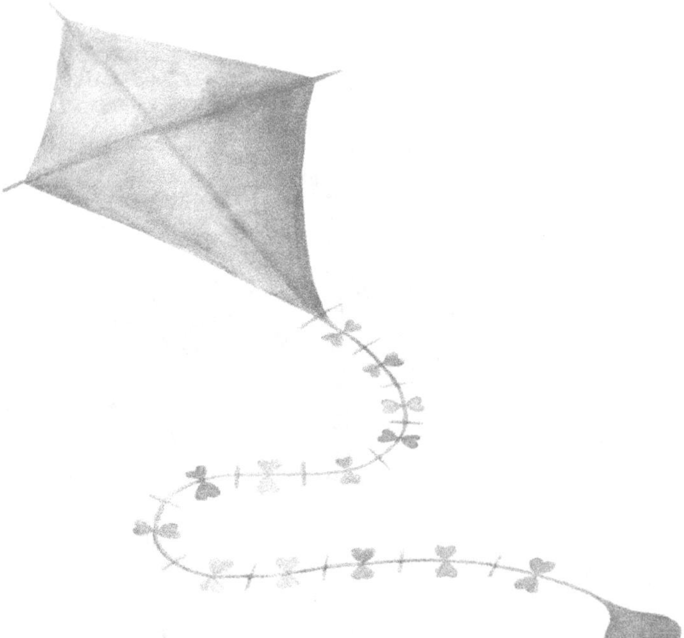

i love you

love you

LOVE

Love

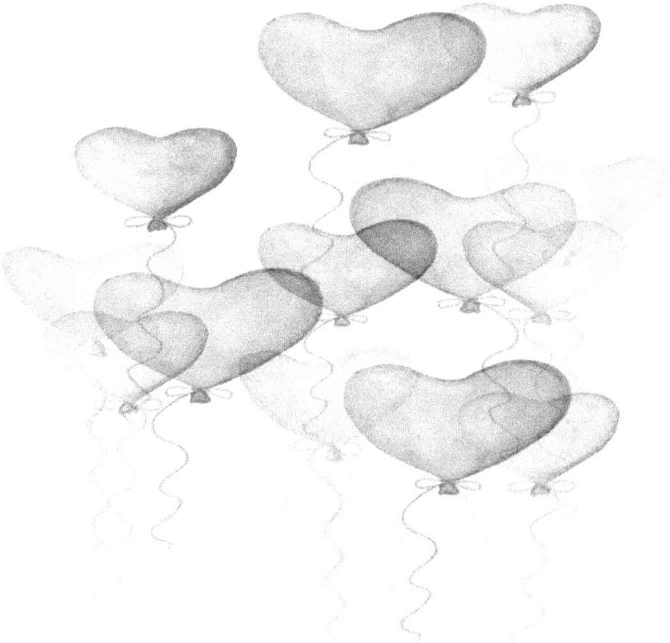

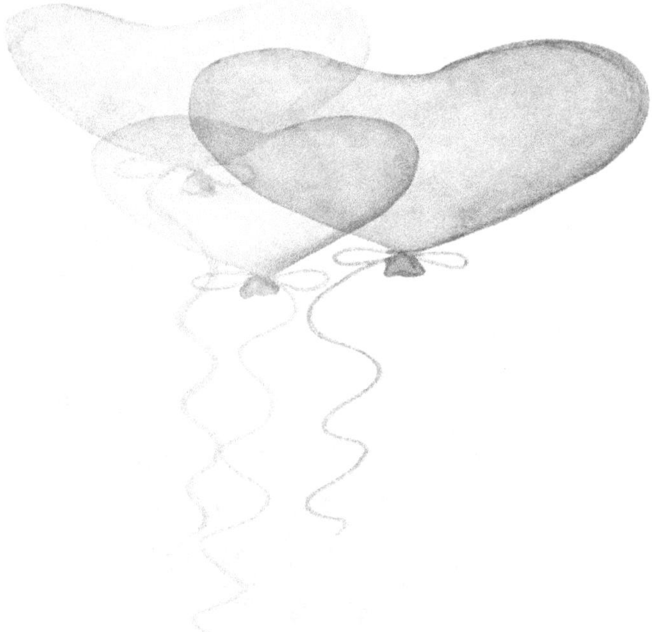

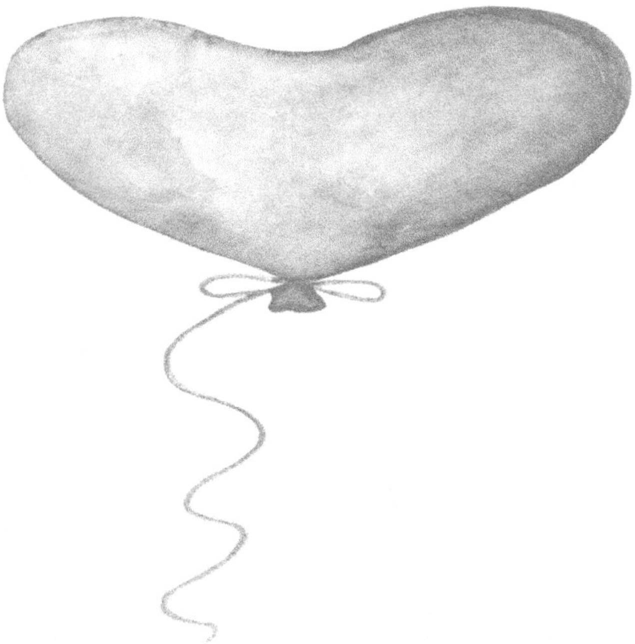

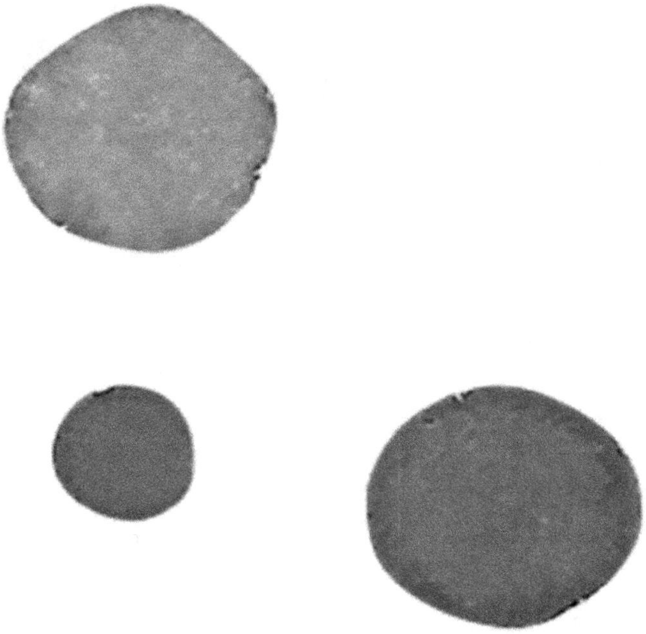

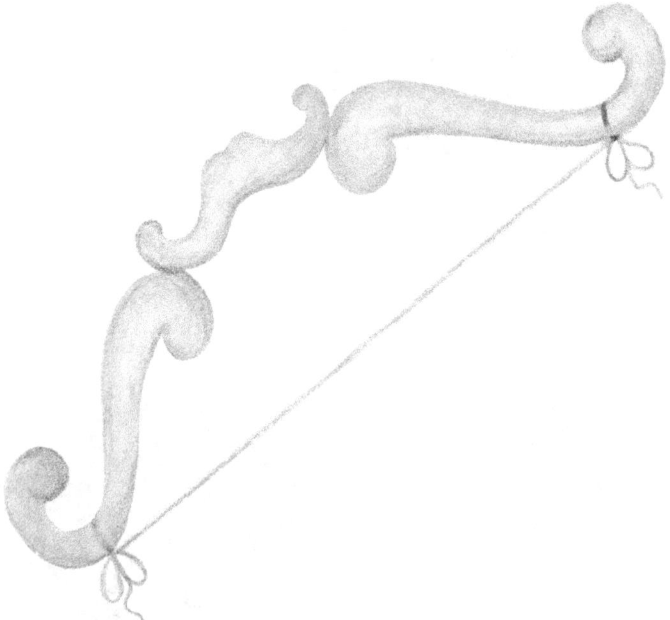

you are loved

love is all you need

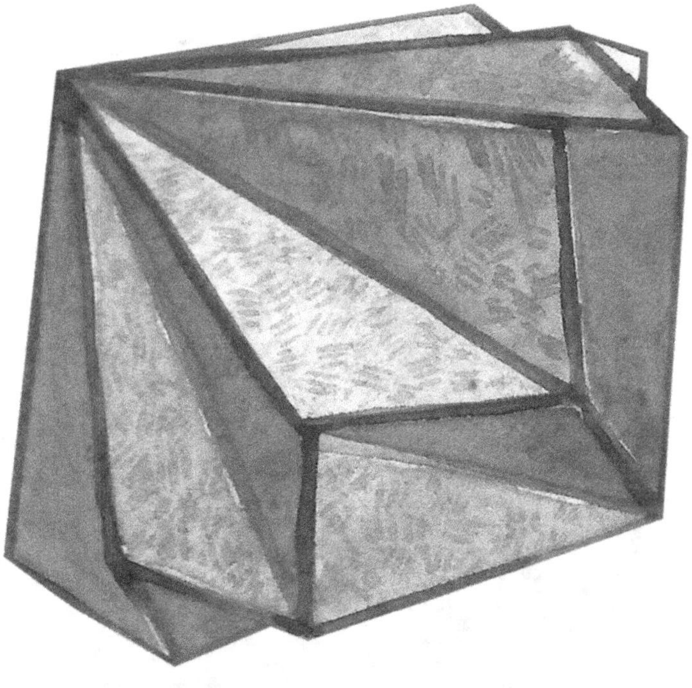

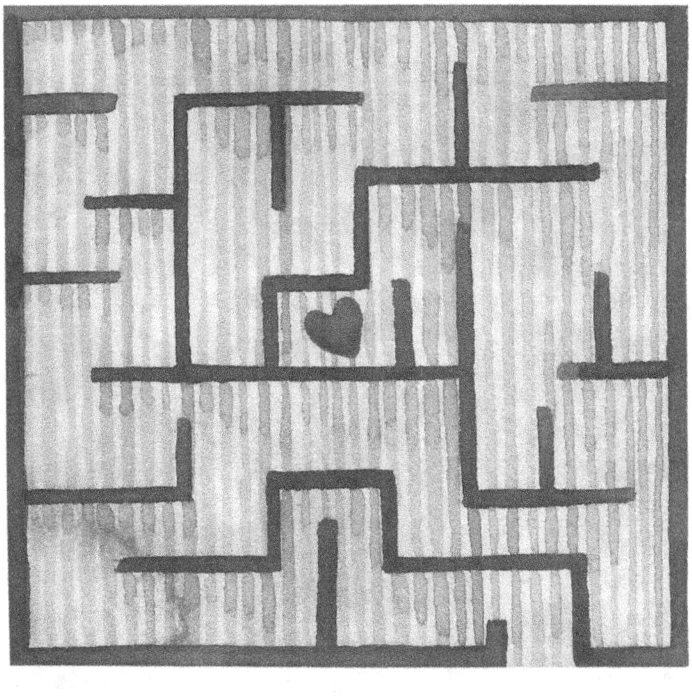

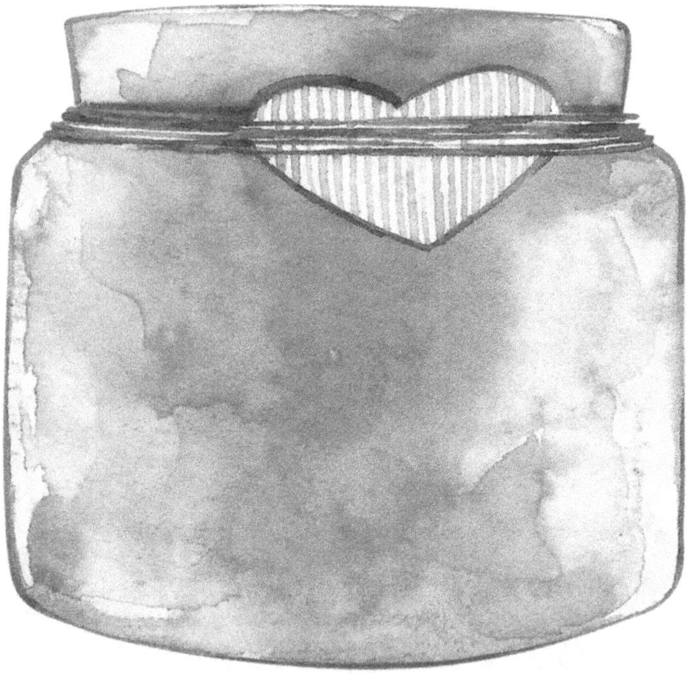

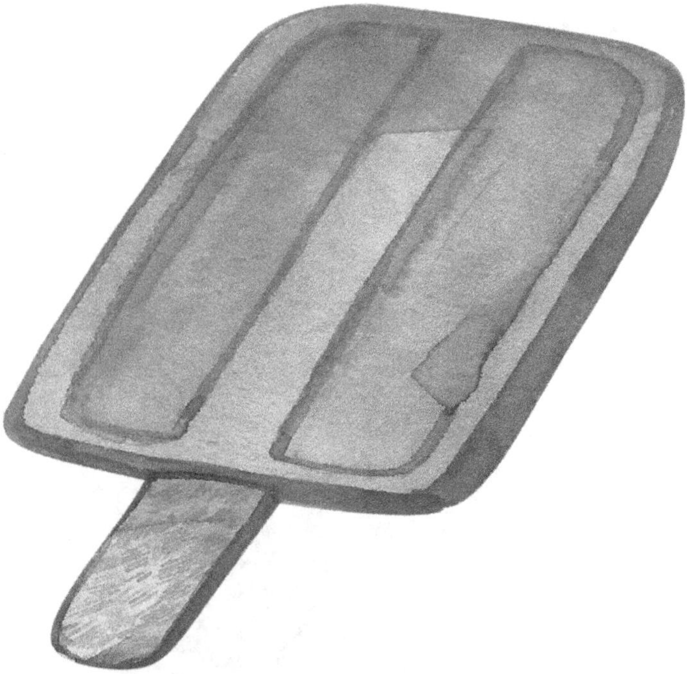

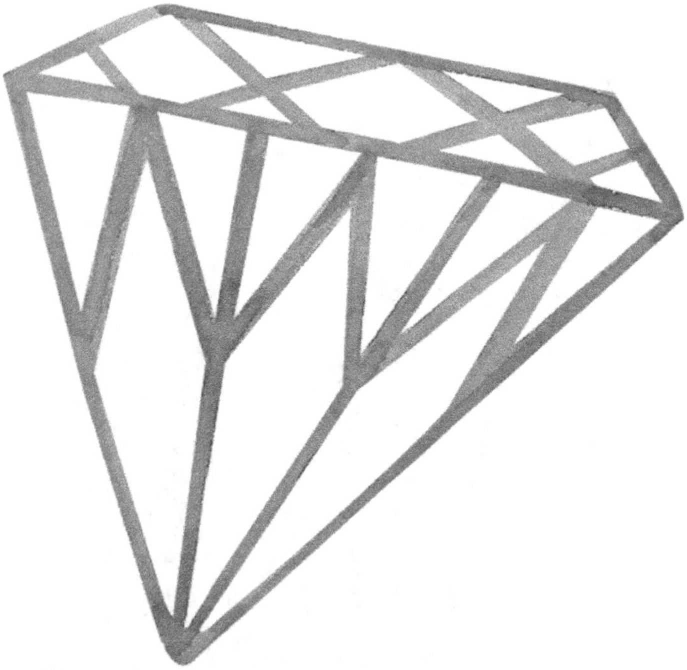

LOVE

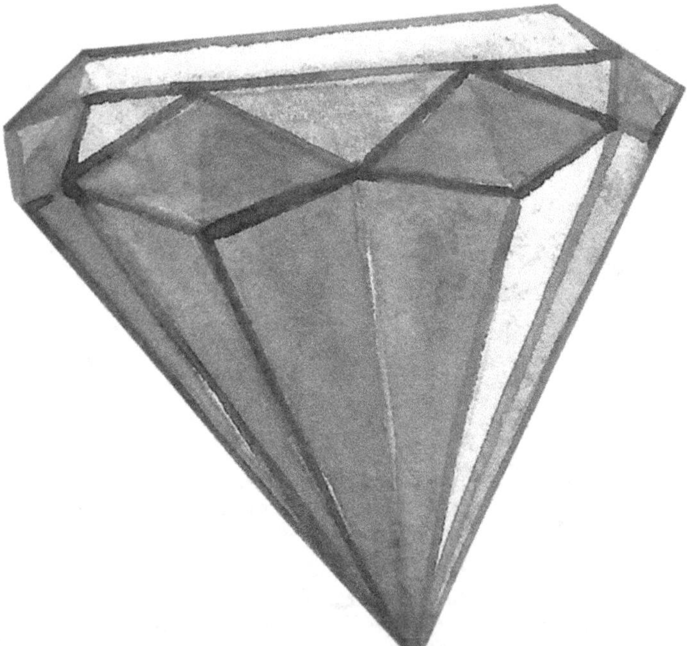

- Acts of Kindness Tracker -

- Acts of Kindness Tracker -

- Acts of Kindness Tracker -

Notes

Notes

Notes

www.ingramcontent.com/pod-product-compliance
Lightning Source LLC
LaVergne TN
LVHW060139080526
838202LV00049B/4028